Molly Wanted a Cute Pony not Naughty

Robyn McRae

Copyright © 2019 by Robyn McRae.

ISBN-9781645507024

All rights reserved. No part of this book may be reproduced or transmitted in any form or by any means, electronic or mechanical, including photocopying, recording, or by any information storage and retrieval system, without permission in writing from the copyright owner.

The views expressed in this work are solely those of the author and do not necessarily reflect the views of the publisher, and the publisher hereby disclaims any responsibility for them.

Matchstick Literary
1-888-306-8885
orders@matchliterary.com

Artist and Author　　　RobynMcRae

"All Molly wanted in the wide world was to ride to Spain. But she had no pony?

"'Why Spain'"?

v

In Spain there were dancing horses.

"Mummy, said they were famous.
She wanted to buy one. Maybe she could buy
A pony for me too"??

"'Molly's best friend Dimiti, said they could dance real high. They were ausome'"

"'Jono, Molly's boyfriend;
he was smart kid, Had had a White horse.'"

"'Of course, Molly wanted one too.'"

"'Would she get a White pony.
Yes she would? Would she ride to Spain?'"

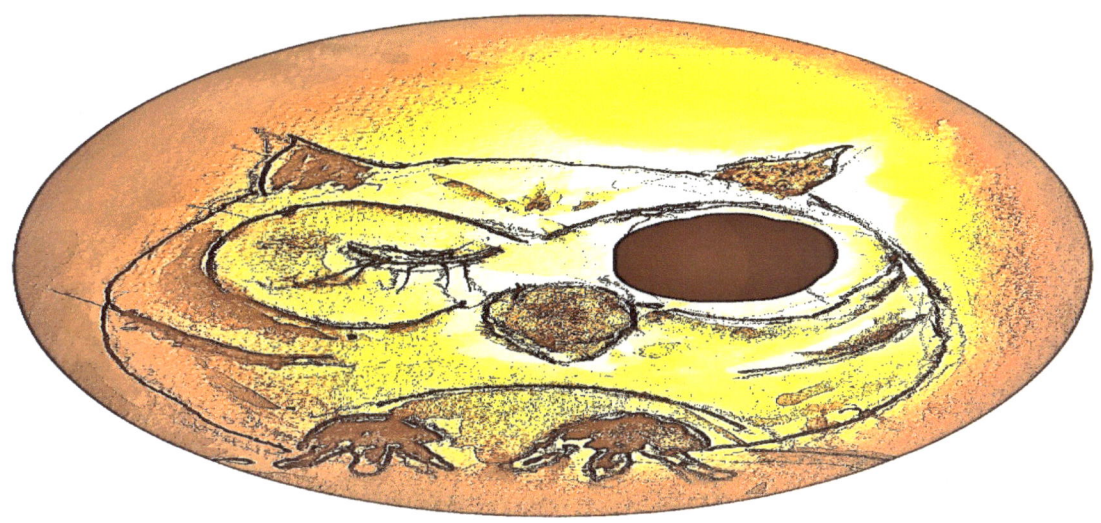

"'No body could stop her..
Not even Billy the Black eyed owl.'"

Chapter 1

"' Billy I will need a pony? Where can I Find a pony ?'"

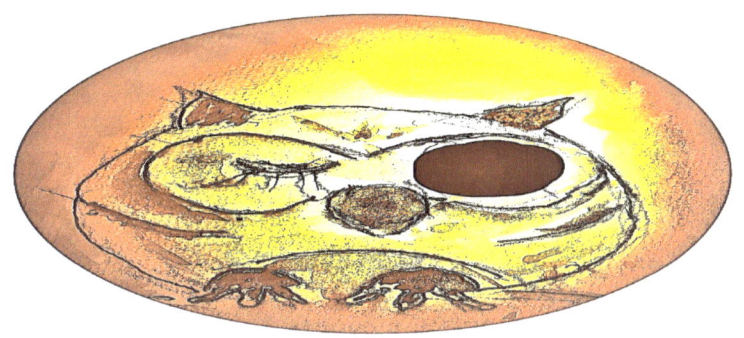

"'I will find a pony Molly. I will fly High and low. What kind of pony '"?

"I want a Spanish pony". A dancing pony."

""You will have to go to Spain".
" Whal !!"".."

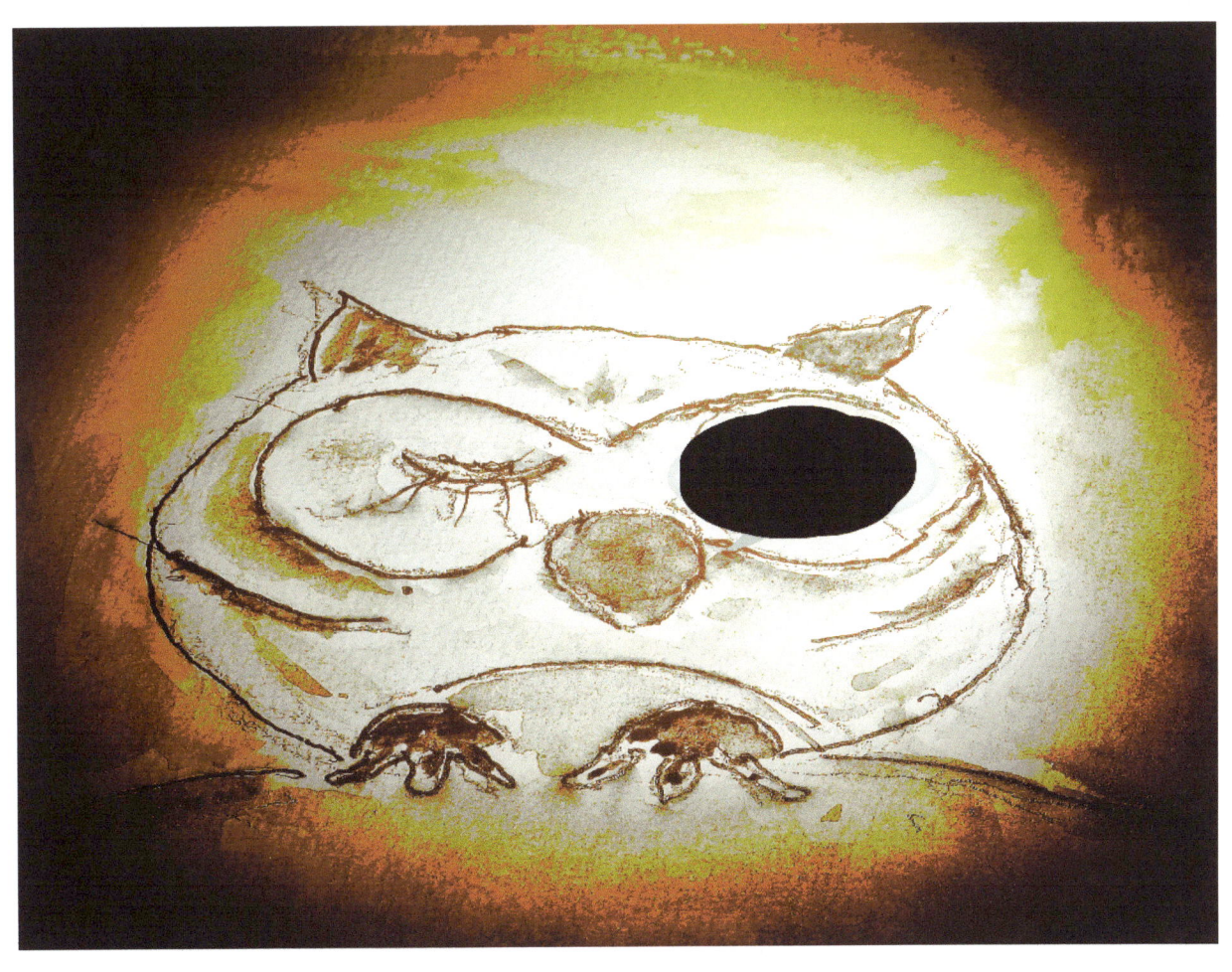

"'Molly UM AH........ "Yes"
"That will be difficult ?...
Its a long way to Spain, from Newzealand"
Do you know where Spain is"?

"No.....?". Molly, Ask Mummy ?
BBilly can we go to Spain"?

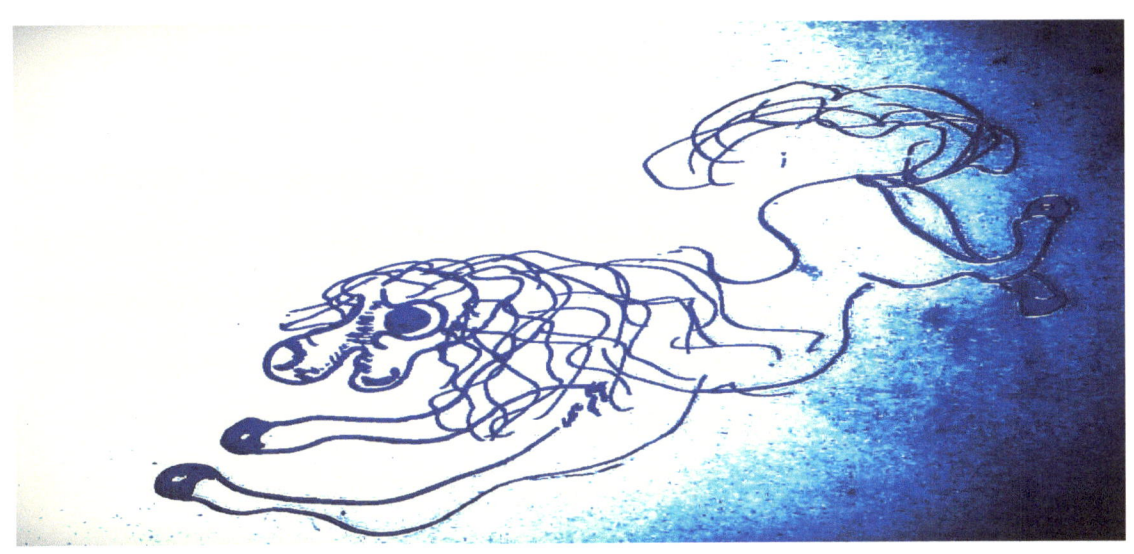

"Then we can get a dancing pony."

"Molly its a long way , from Newzealand".

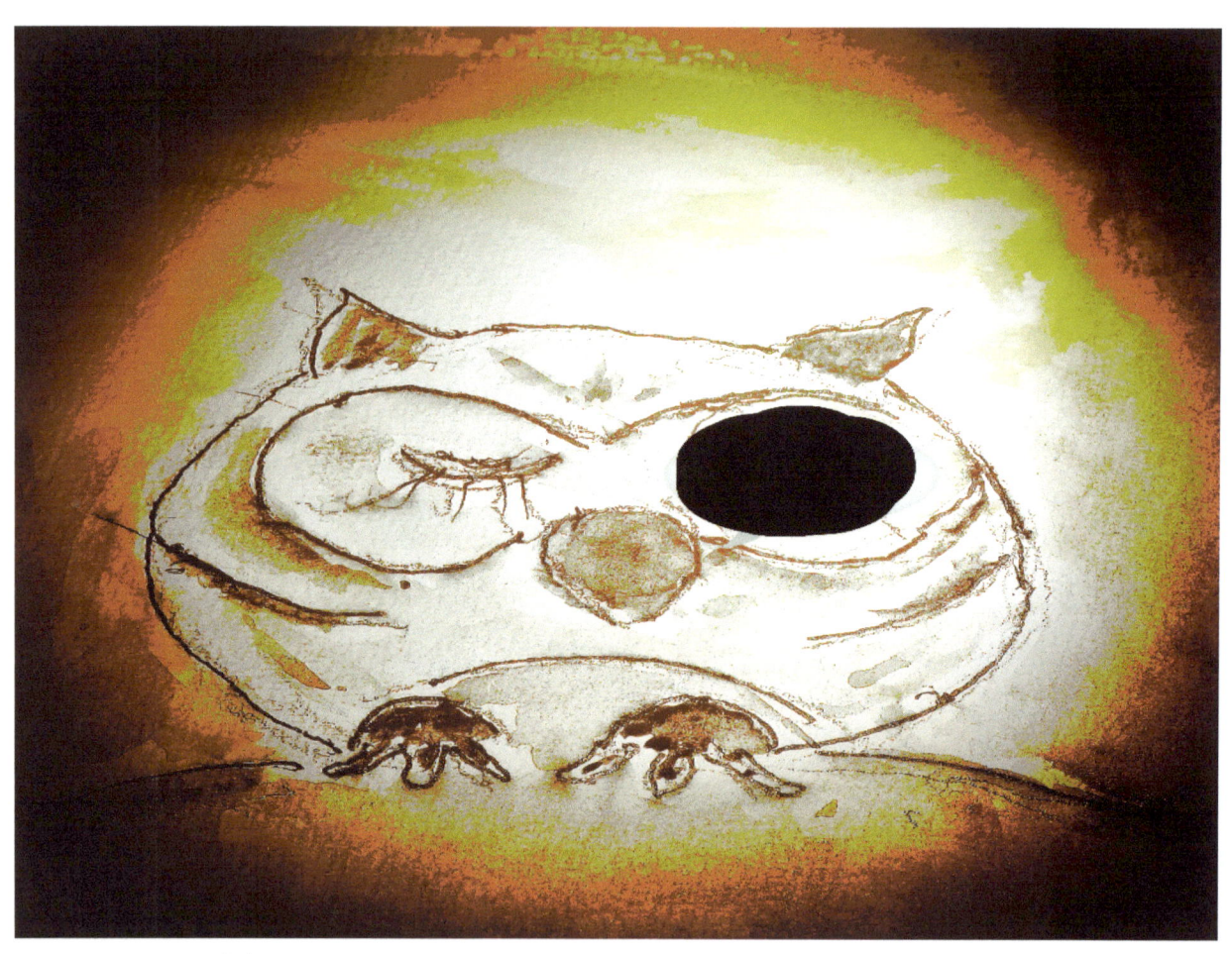

"You will have to go on a big, big aeroplane. "Whal !!....."""

It will cost lots of money.
'Are you paying the   aeroplane?"
"NO I AM NOT " ?........

"The plane leaves at sun rise. So we will have to find some money quick. Molly are you paying?

" O.K.... Mummy won't mind ?"'
"'MOLLY ?.......
Are you sure"?
"You better ask Mummy"?

"Mummy said no........""""""
WHAT NOW ?"

CHAPTER 2

Molly; ride to spain its free

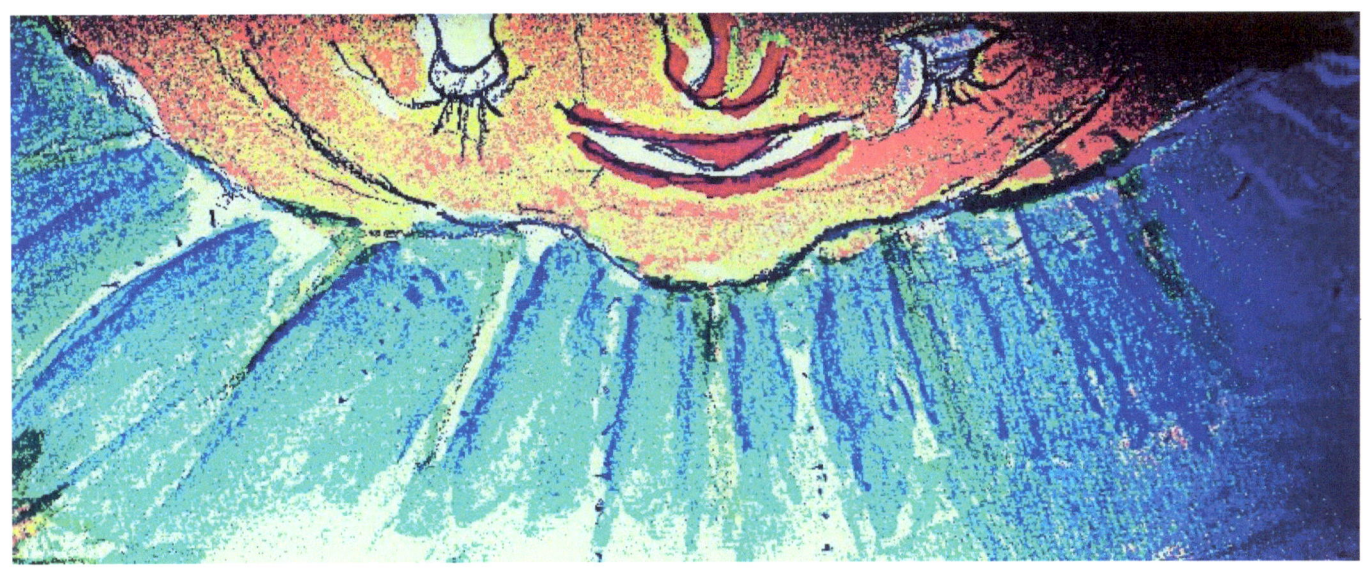

SUNNY SPAIN

"Lets get a White pony just like the

SPANISH PONIES"

HE MUST BE cUTE.

"What do you think he is drinking?"

"NO SUNBATHING
There will be no time for that.
Lets get to Sunny Spain first".

It cannot be lazy.

"It mus be good, not NAUGHTY!!"

It It must like It must must like adventure.
"'You will get plenty of that"

"Its got to be tough"!
"It will snow. It will rain. The wind will blow".
Do you still want to go ?"

"Sure do! Daddy said .... "Never turn back". Climb every mountain; ford every stream and then you will find your dream."

L "Lets get a White pony that can dance."

,,,,,"Um Ah?....
I will get the right kind of pony

Just wait and see......"
"NEIGH"""".....
"Molly have you heard the latest gossip" Whats the goss Lucky.
They say, that you want a White pony to ride to Spain"""".

BAD LUCK.
You are not White. You have no spots and can you dance "?

"Lucky, good luck....... Have some hay."

"Lucky, good luck……Have some hay."

WHO ARE THEY ??
Pumpkin our ginger cat would meow
Cocker Spaniel would yelp the Imp gang song.
Practical Prickly would run at top speed. (for a Hedgehog) !!!

Practical Prickly, he would carry the IMP GANG flag.

Pumpie loved to fish. "Does your daddy go fishing

fishing?"
"Lets go to the circus, we might see your pony there.

"Woopee!"
Can I have this one? Its White and it can dance too
But it has no spots "!!?

"Do you like spots"? "Yes I love spots."

"Just one spot will do ?....."

"Mummy I want to ride to Spain but I have no pony.
Moll'.......? You cannot go. Its a long way, a long way.....
Molly you need a pony. O.K......
Its your birthday tomorrow ?...?"

"Mummy I want to ride to Spain but I have no pony.
Moll'.......? You cannot go. Its a long way, a long way.....
Molly you need a pony. O.K......
Its your birthday tomorrow ?...?"

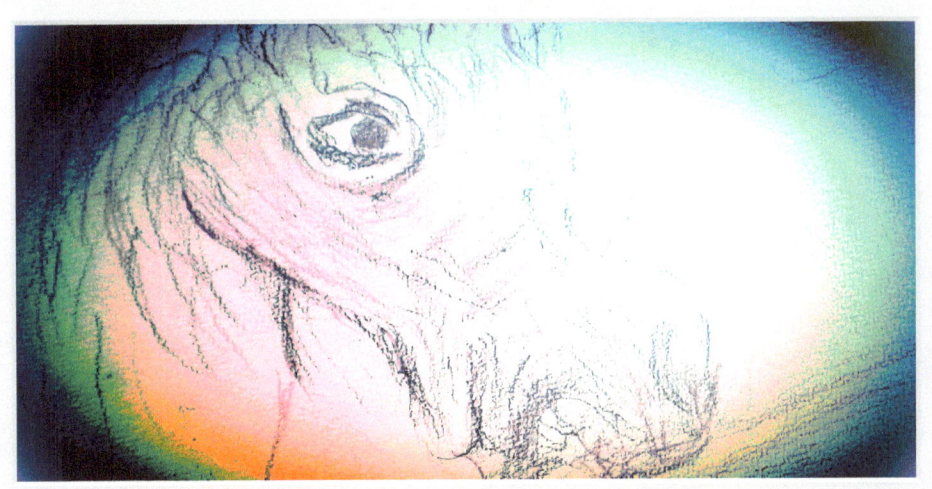

To my best friend

Life is like a song. You just
need to learn to sing it

From

To my best friend

Life is like a song. You just
need to learn to sing it

We are all delicate, precious and beautiful.
When you look at...
How perfect the delicate, precious rose flower is.
Then maybe, then you will... touch much more gently and lovingly,
with appreciation... as you appreciate the Rose.

After all we are all delicate precious and
beautiful like the Rose.

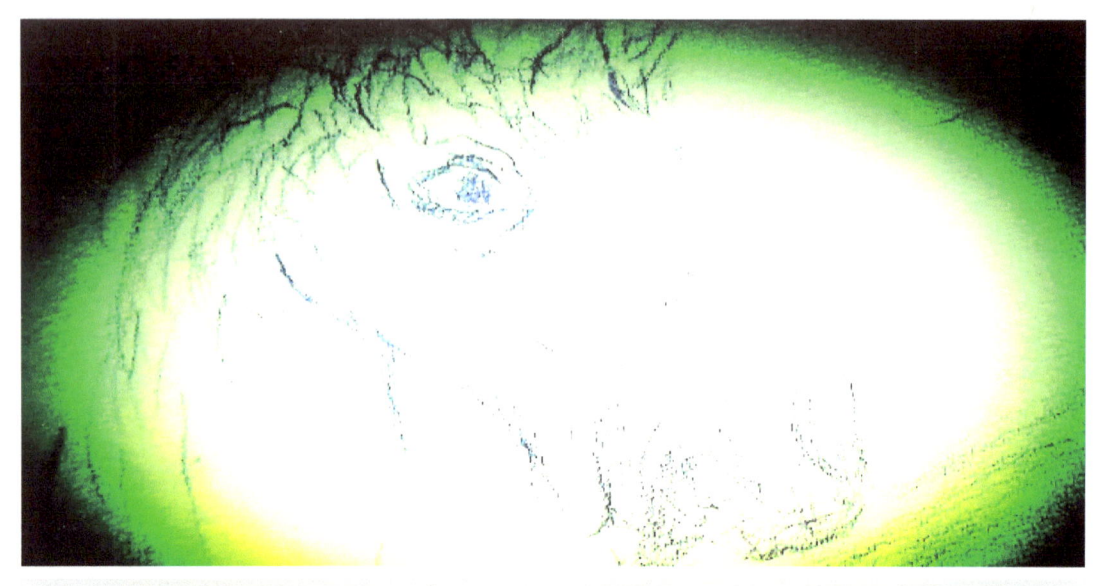
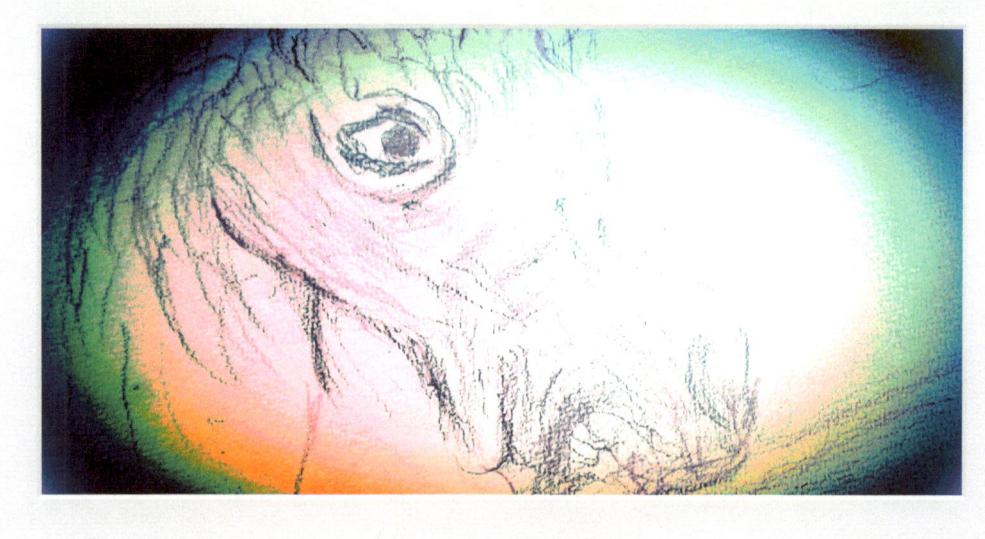

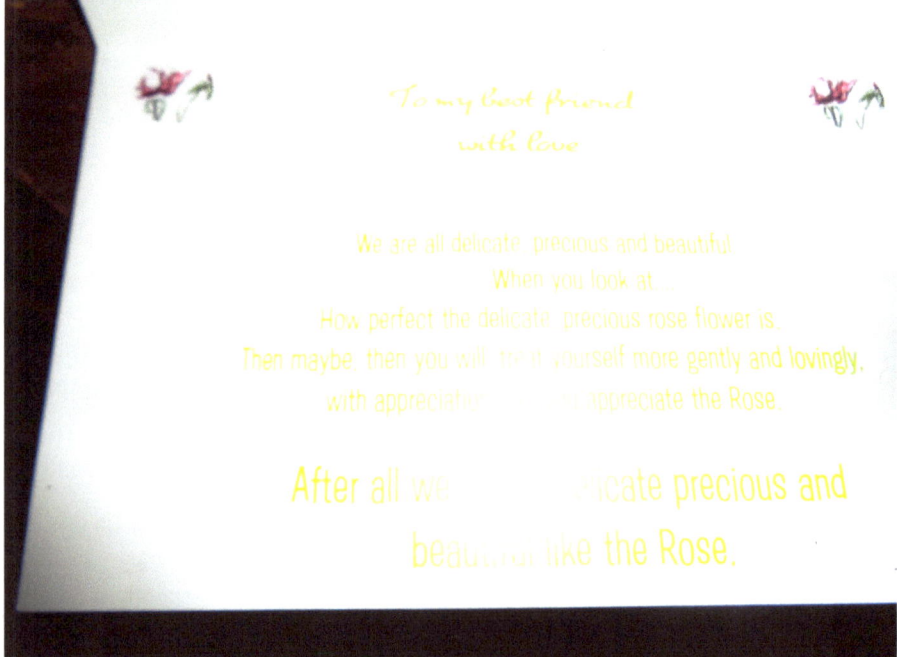

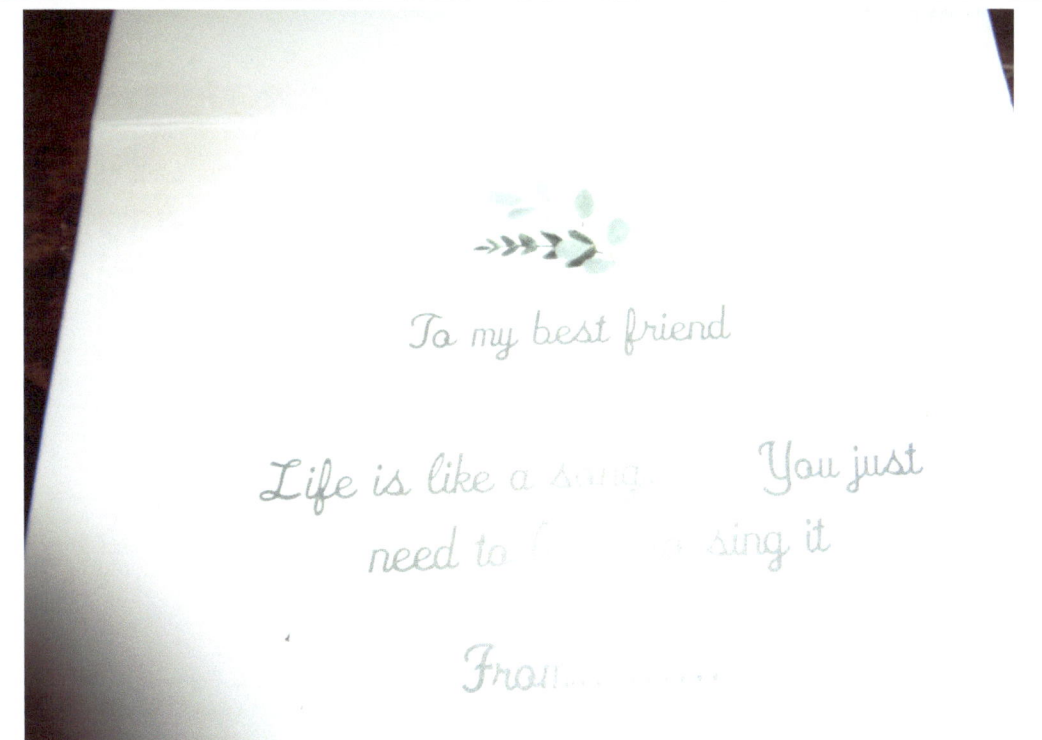

To my best friend

Life is like a song... You just
need to find it, sing it

From

To my best friend

Life is like a song. You just need to learn to sing it.

From...

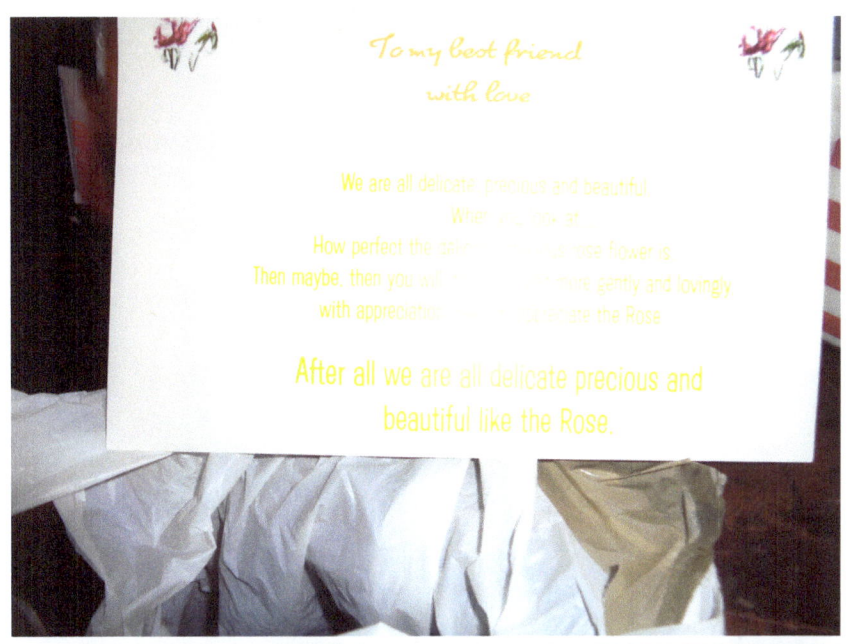

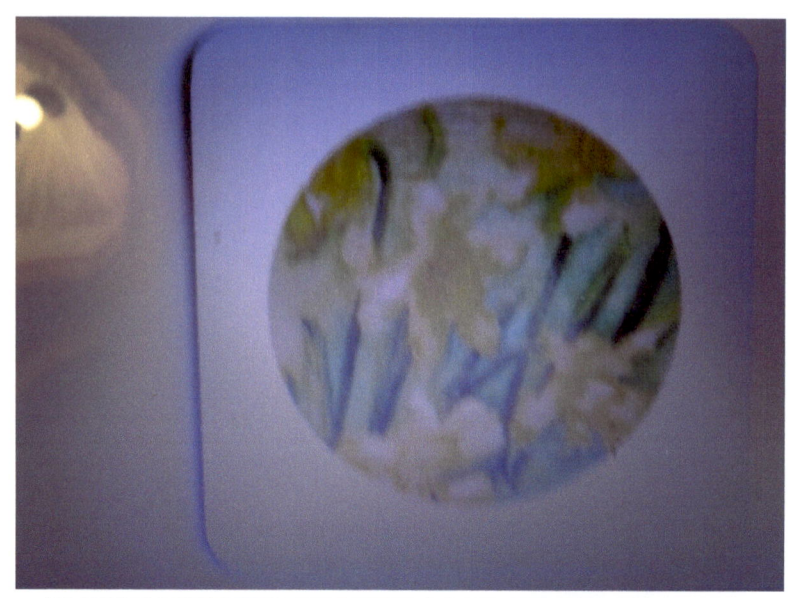

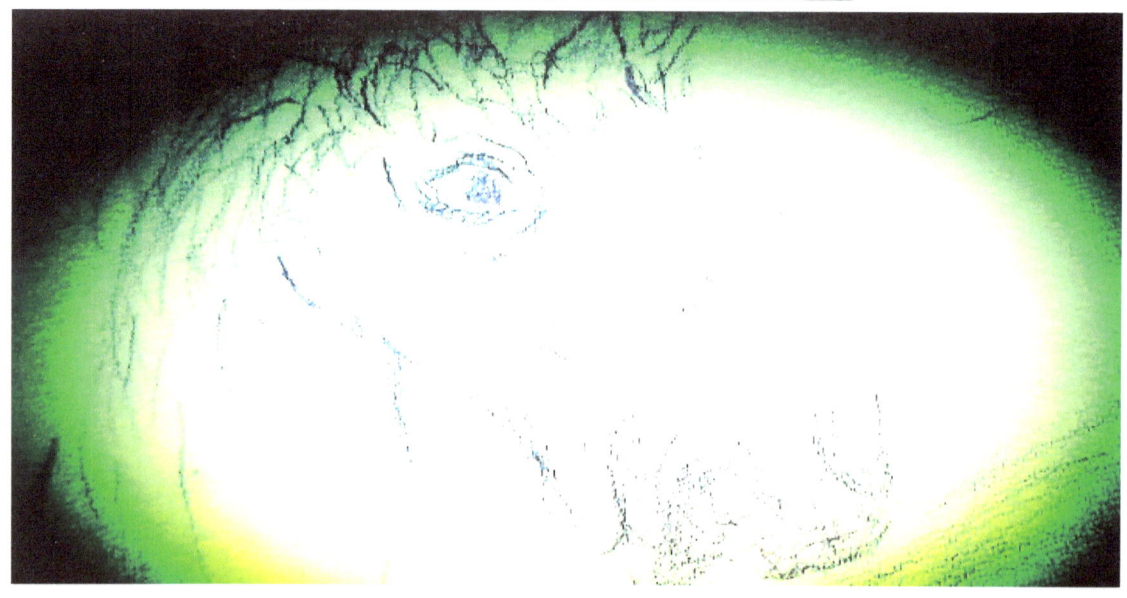

Yes, Billy....... I want a Spanish pony.

"' Well good.. When we get the pony.

Look he's got lots and lots of apples.
Molly and Prickly would not starve.

Chapter 3

LLets get my pony, Billy, ...

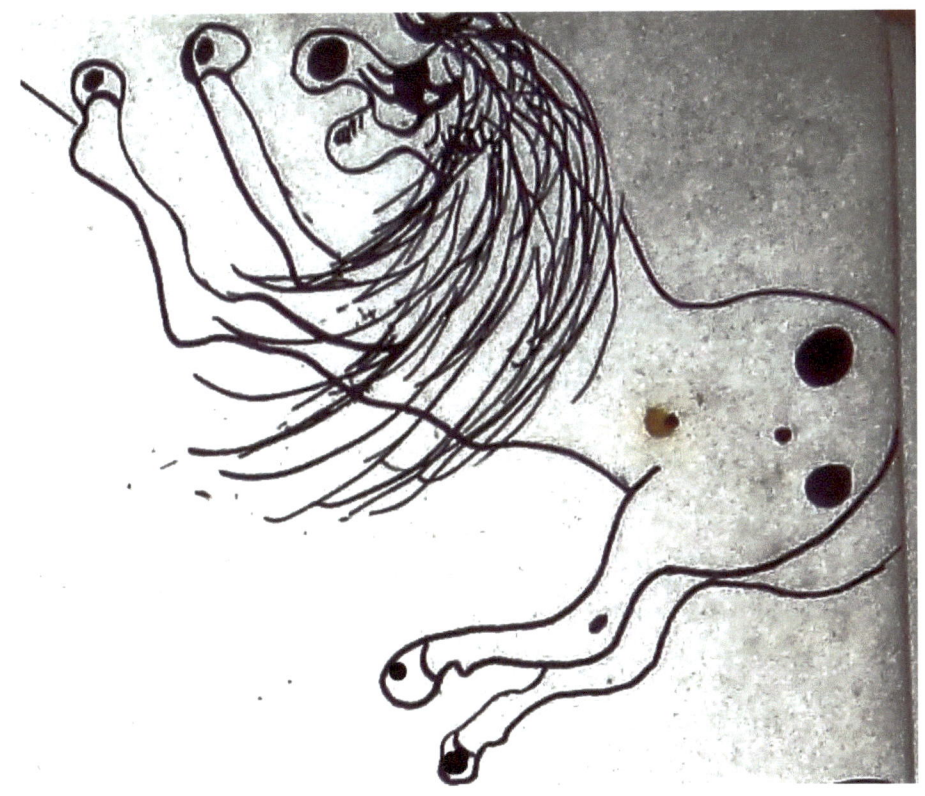

""Lets go to the circus.
Maybe your pony will be there?

What about a different pony
Do you like spots?"
"Yes one spot will do."

Mummy I want to ride to Spain.
Molly, you cannot go to Spain! Molly its a
Long, long way to Spain! And gosh, you need a pony?
Ah ?........UM...

"Did you ask Daddy for my pony"?

" OOh.....SORRY Molly....I forgot !!"
" Its alright Mummy. I will ask Daddy."

"DADDY Can I have a pony ??...
I WILL LOVE IT I WILL FEED IT APPLES AND

GROOM HER COAT SO ITS SHINY"

Its your birthday tomorrow."
" I wonder if Daddy got her a."…….pony ?".

Grace the good fairy fluttered in.
"' What do you want dear Molly"??......
" I want a pony, a spotted pony. I want to ride to Spain,
To see the White dancing horses"'

Molly, what you want you shall get !

Abradabbricca !!!
The next day arrived.
A pony with one spot.
"Thankyou Grace"'

Molly tried to pick a Apple from the old Oak tree.
Actually, our Ginger cat did. Her friend Issie Wissie just watched.
"'Down they came......... LOTS AND LOTS ,OF Apples "!
"BOOM !""""

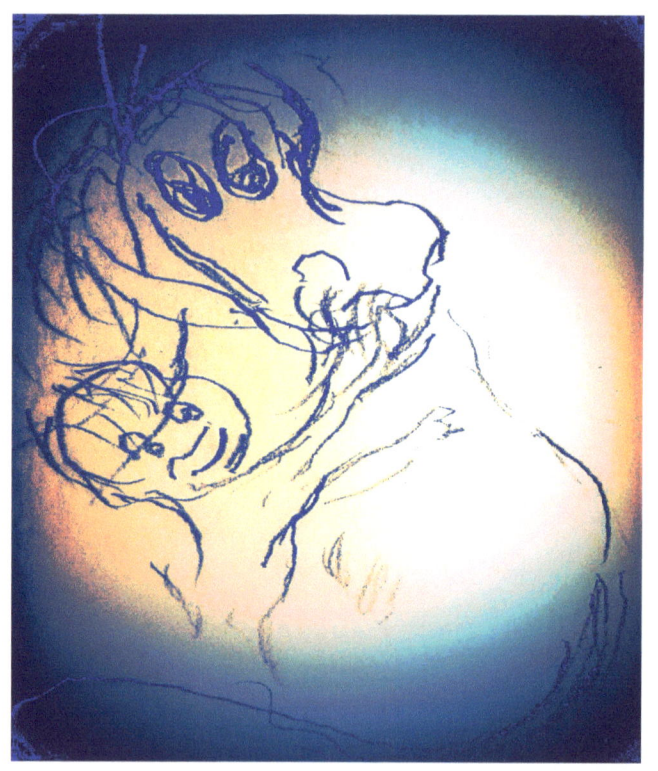

Molly gave her new friend a great big Red apple.

"I She neighed,"""" quietly.....""
It was a funny noise but Molly liked it..

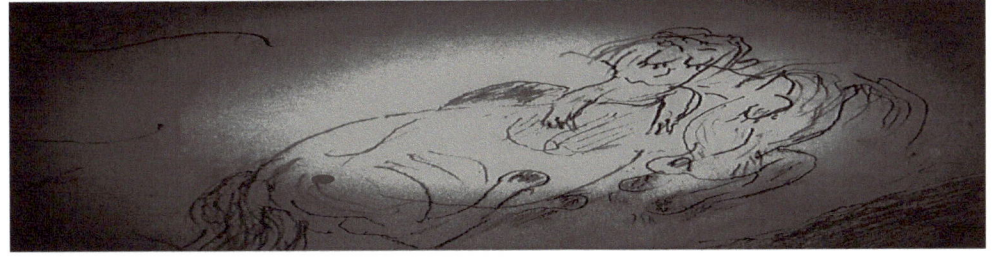

We all loved her. She was so cuddly...

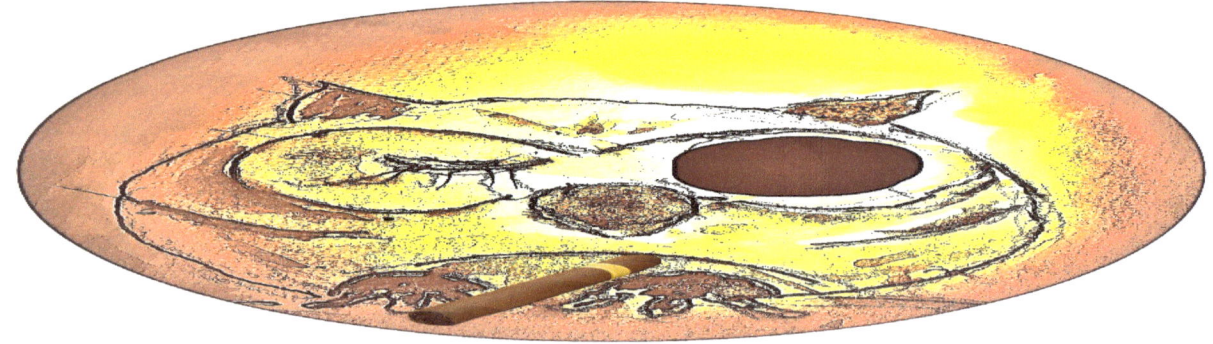

Prickly our Hedgehog grunted. ""Call her Imp, she looks ....

NAUGHTY"?

Molly screamed ," look shes got Mummies favourite Red Roses.
No nooo no Naughty Naughty Imp"""".........

So she gobbled all the Roses up. Mummy was cross..... "! I bet she was !"!
So we called her "NAUGHTY IMP !!! She gave a wicked smile "!!

"' Silly name but……she was naughty"…
"Ponies can be naughty but you must always forgive.
"' Then they will be good…."'

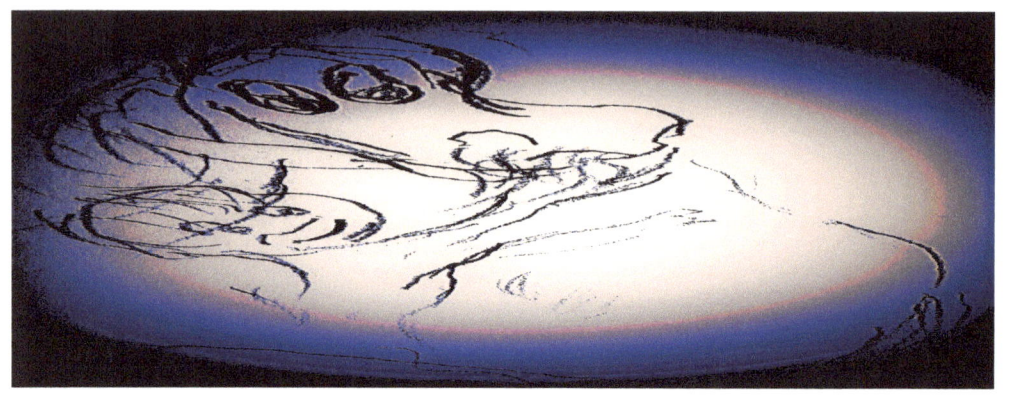

Molly do you want a ride.? "' Sure do……….? Do you buck"'?
" Molly I will be good…""Ponies always are good when riders trust them"…..

"My friends said you needed a pony to take
you to see the dancing ponies."
"' Yes"' ?
" It must beable to dance…. Can you dance.?
Can you do the Spanish trot? "'"' No Sort of
? But my cousins in Spain can…."'

"'Yes'"?
" It must beable to dance.... Can you dance."'?
Can you do the Spanish trot? "' "' No Sort of ? But my cousins in

Sunny Spain can...."'

"Lets go find your coz's in sunny Spain
Lets go Imp. Come on Imp"'.....

"' Molly I have no bridal.......?
I will need a bridal..."'

So Daddy gave Molly a brand new Black bridal.
leather bridal. ...... "Nice and Strong too"!

"1"Thankyou Daddy. I can ride to Spain now !

"I won't get lost. See I have a map and a flag...
I will meet you there ?"

'"SEE YOU........"

"I will meet you there ?"
I will buy tickets for you and Mummy to fly......."'

to Sunny Spain ?

Daddie always said........ "' Climb every mountain ford every stream and there you will find dancing ponies ......"

"'Do you think
Molly will get to Spain ??.....'"

read on Naughty Imp goes to Spain
with the Imp gang

ARTIST and TEXT Robyne McRae / Cory

Books out in bookshops, You Tube Facebook and Amazon
and more Nationally and Internationally.

Printed and published on .... /3/2020
by Matchstickliterary.com USA

suggestion for......
Naughty Impiti goes to Spain.
With the Imp gang. "Who are they "?

Flowers. No Imp no..........

So we called him Naughty Imp. Imp grinned !!

Right said Molly. Let's have a party !! A welcolm

To the den for Naughty Imp.

I will make a cake Pumpie, you can ice it.
But you cannot lick it.
Shebs, you can pass the Horsey Aid.
But don"t drop it.
Owl, you can do the speech. The welcolm Imp speech,
But Billy don"t forget it and Prickly you can get
Lots and lots of nuts. Crunch.........

Sheba did not drop the horsey Aid. Naughty Imp